D1332788

Restoring Venice

The Church of the Madonna dell'Orto

Restoring Venice

The Church of the Madonna dell'Orto

Edited by Ashley Clarke
Vice-Chairman, Venice in Peril Fund
and Philip Rylands

With contributions by
Francesco Valcanover
Renato Padoan
Joyce Plesters
& Lorenzo Lazzarini
Kenneth Hempel

Paul Elek London

All that intelligence and hard work created in times past, intelligence and hard work have now to preserve.

Goethe, *Italian Journey*, trans. W. H. Auden & Elizabeth Mayer.

Published in Great Britain 1977 by
Paul Elek Ltd
54–58 Caledonian Road, London
N1 9RN

Designed by Harold Bartram

ISBN 0 236 40080 0

Printed by
The Garden City Press Limited
Letchworth, Hertfordshire
SG6 1JS

Contents

Foreword

The achievement which this book commemorates was made possible by the intervention of the British *Italian Art and Archives Rescue Fund* – now succeeded by the Venice in Peril Fund – and the generosity of its benefactors, in conjunction with funds given by the Italian government.

Although the original authorization for the restoration of the Madonna dell'Orto was given by the then *Soprintendente ai Monumenti* the work was actually carried out under the overall authority and guidance of Arch. Renato Padoan, who has been kind enough to write a Preface to the architectural section.

For the passage concerning the restoration of the paintings by Tintoretto in the church, I am most grateful to the *Soprintendente alle Gallerie ed Opere d'Arte*, Dr Francesco Valcanover, under whose authority the restoration laboratory of San Gregorio operates. His encouragement and intervention at certain crucial moments were an important element in the success achieved, and his help and advice in the preparation of this book have been invaluable.

Among many other men and women who have given their labours and their knowledge to carry forward this restoration and its documentation, I am much indebted to Arch. Marco Bisà, the member of the *Soprintendenza ai Monumenti* who was directly in charge of the restoration of the fabric of the Madonna dell'Orto. He prepared the first draft of the architectural section of this book, selected many of the photographs, provided material for many of the captions, and has kindly allowed me to use one of his architectural drawings.

I am also greatly indebted to Miss Joyce Plesters for her authoritative essay, jointly with Dr Lorenzo Lazzarini, on the technical aspects of restoring the Tintorettos. Their contribution to this book is all the more valuable in that it was Miss Plesters who originally set up the Scientific department of the San Gregorio laboratory, where Dr Lorenzo Lazzarini has been working ever since.

The cleaning and restoration of the *St Christopher and Child* were executed by Mr Kenneth Hempel of the Victoria and Albert Museum, and his assistant Signorina Giulia Musumeci, who did a period of training there. I am most grateful to Mr Hempel for his report on this important sculpture – the first substantial work in Istrian stone to be restored in Venice. My thanks are also due to Signorina Musumeci for much vital technical advice.

1 The Madonna dell'Orto, before restoration

Both Superintendents have generously given permission for the reproduction of a number of photographs from their respective archives. A special word of thanks is due to the building contractor, Signor Enzo Fassi, for some valuable photographs taken in the earliest stages of the operation showing the degree of disintegration and pollution with which we were faced. I also owe thanks to Sarah Quill who contributed photographs and to Sir James Richards who very kindly gave assistance and advice during the final stages of the book's production.

Thousands of people have directly or indirectly contributed to the restoration of the Madonna dell'Orto and it was for the sake of those supporters who could not share at first hand the pleasure of observing the actual work that the idea to prepare this description was first considered. It has since grown into an important record of some successful solutions of the problems to be faced in such a sweeping restoration of a building and its works of art: problems which will have to be faced repeatedly in the future to save many other Venetian buildings in similar straits. But the success of this project and its good effects are not only to be found in the contrasts observable in the 'before' and 'after' pictures, for it has done more than save a precious monument, it has indeed created a monument of international co-operation and interest in Venice; and for me, now, that is what the Madonna dell'Orto has come to stand for.

Ashley Clarke
Vice-Chairman
Venice in Peril Fund

A Note on the Contributors

Sir Ashley Clarke, GCMG, GCVO, British Ambassador to Italy, 1953–62, and Chairman of the Italian Art and Archives Rescue Fund, 1966–70.

Dr Francesco Valcanover, art historian and *Soprintendente alle Gallerie ed Opere d'Arte*, Venice.

Arch. Renato Padoan, *Soprintendente ai Monumenti*, Venice.

Miss Joyce Plesters, Senior Scientific Officer, the National Gallery, London; and Dr Lorenzo Lazzarini, Scientific Officer, *Soprintendenza alle Gallerie ed Opere d'Arte*, Venice.

Kenneth Hempel, OBE, Restorer I, Sculpture Restoration, Victoria and Albert Museum, London.

Introduction

As the departing visitor crosses the lagoon towards Marco Polo airport, the
last dark sentinel he sees in the northern skyline of Venice is the *campanile* of
the Church of the Madonna dell'Orto. Like a tall cypress in a most un-Tuscan
landscape, it is also the first monument to beckon him back on his return (see
plate 2). And there is a certain aptness in this, for when the British *Italian Art
and Archives Rescue Fund* (the predecessor of the Venice in Peril Fund)
selected this church, it became the first Venetian monument to be
comprehensively restored – that is to say, in its fabric, sculptures and
paintings – since the disastrous flood of November 1966. It pioneered a series
of such restorations sponsored by foreign, as well as Italian, funds for saving
Venice.

The first church on the site of the Madonna dell'Orto was founded around
1350 by Fra Tiberio da Parma, General of the monastic order of the
Umiliati, although there are traces of an earlier monastic foundation on newly
reclaimed land from the end of the twelfth century. The church was
originally dedicated to St Christopher and officially still remains so. But very
early the name was changed in popular parlance to the Madonna dell'Orto.
The diarist, Marin Sanudo, in some notes for a history of Venice, related how
a certain sculptor, Giovanni de Santis, carved a monumental *Virgin and Child*

2 View of Venice from the lagoon
near Murano

9

3 The main door of the church, c. 1910

for the Church of Santa Maria Formosa, which the Prior of that church rejected. The sculpture was left, unpaid for, in an orchard (*orto*) near the Church of San Cristoforo until reports reached the Bishop of Venice, Paolo Foscari, that a radiant light shone nightly over the stone Virgin's head. By the Bishop's order, she was robed in Alexandrine velvet, and on 18th June 1377 was carried into the Church of San Cristoforo which has been known since then as the Madonna dell'Orto. When Giovanni de Santis died in 1384 he was buried in the church. The miraculous *Virgin and Child* can be seen today, much restored with plaster, in the Chapel of San Mauro, adjacent to the Sacristy (see plate 27).

There seems to have been something seriously amiss with the foundations of the first building since a complete reconstruction had to be undertaken around 1399. The most likely explanation is that, being newly reclaimed from the lagoon, the ground under the church had subsided unevenly. Work continued, not without further complications, during most of the fifteenth century. The definitive restoration took place in 1473. In 1461 the order of

San Giorgio in Alga, to which the popular San Lorenzo Giustinian had belonged, was confirmed as successor to the *Umiliati*, who had been expelled by Pope Pius II on the advice of the *Maggior Consiglio* because of their lax habits (*rilassatezza di costumi*). As so often, the moral reform of the monastery went hand in hand with architectural renovation.

Considering all things, it is remarkable that the result is such a perfect example of Venetian Gothic, not in the least spoilt by the backward glance at the Romanesque in the multiplication of niches on the façade,* nor by the salute to the Renaissance in the scalloped pediment and Corinthian columns of the main portal (see plate 3). In essence the façade must be as originally designed by Fra Tiberio (although the windows, which are crowded against the cornice, are of a later date) who clearly based his plans on the monastic churches of the Frari and Santi Giovanni e Paolo. The twelve *Apostles* in the niches are attributed to the Delle Masegne brothers, the *St Christopher and Child* over the main doorway to Bartolomeo Bon, and the *Virgin* (see plate 4) and *Angel Gabriel* above the doorposts are attributed to the young Antonio Rizzo.†

* Corbel tables, under the cornice of the façade as well as the north and south walls, constitute another Romanesque element.

† The five *Virtues* in the aedicules that crown the façade date from 1719 and were brought from the suppressed church of Santo Stefano di Murano in 1845 during a restoration of the Madonna dell'Orto.

4 *The Virgin Annunciate*, attributed to Antonio Rizzo

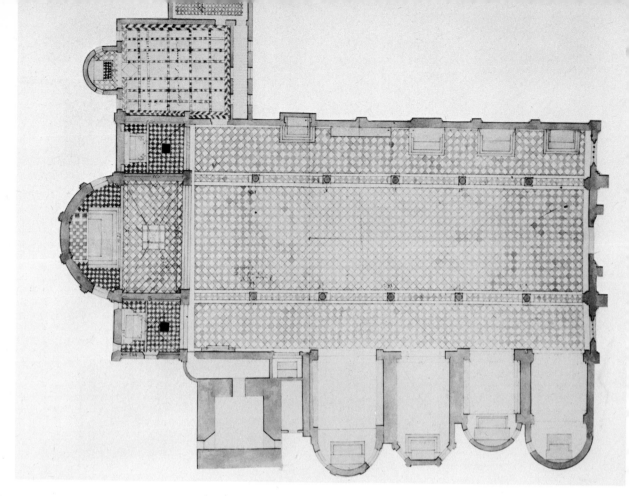

5 Ground plan of the church. From a drawing made in 1868

The interior is simple and spacious, consisting of a nave and two side-aisles divided by columns of Turkish marble, a semi-circular vaulted apse and side-chapels but no transepts, and further side-chapels off the north aisle (see plate 5). The chief glory of the interior is the collection of paintings by Tintoretto, including the immense *Last Judgment* and the *Adoration of the Golden Calf* on either side of the chancel. The subjects of these paintings, which are admonitions against errors of faith, reflect, according to Anna Palluchini, the spread of the Counter-Reformation to Venice in the early 1560s. Tintoretto seems also to have frescoed the ceiling of the Valier Chapel, but nothing remains of this. The precise dates of Tintoretto's works are not known, but it is recounted that in punishment for some solecism he was shut up in the Madonna dell'Orto by order of the Bishop, who refused to allow him out until he had suitably decorated what was his own place of worship. All of Tintoretto's canvases were restored in 1968–69 with funds from the Italian State. Tintoretto was eventually buried in the church, and a memorial to him has been placed in the chapel to the right of the high altar. Apart from the Tintorettos, the church contains numerous works of art including an early *Madonna and Child* by Giovanni Bellini, and a *St John the Baptist with four saints*, one of Cima da Conegliano's masterpieces. The Bellini Madonna is undergoing restoration at present after being damaged in an attempted theft, and the Cima was restored in 1962 on the occasion of an exhibition of Cima's work in Treviso.

In 1556, the ceiling of the nave was decorated with perspective paintings by Cristoforo and Stefano Rosa of Brescia, which Vasari, in 1568, described as follows:

> . . . a colonnade of double twisted columns on the flat ceiling like those of the Porta Santa at St Peter's in Rome; the which, rising from some projecting cornices, form in the church a superb corridor with cross-vaults; it is in the middle of the church with fine fore-shortenings which astound those who see them, and the ceiling, which is flat, looks deep; above all, it is adorned by a fine variety of cornices, masks, festoons, and some figures which most richly decorate the whole work . . . (from *Le Vite*, Part III, the life of Garofalo.)

The success of this project, no trace of which has survived, earned the painters the commission to decorate the ceiling of the vestibule of the old Marcian Library; the painting survives today and gives an idea of how the nave of the Madonna dell'Orto once looked.

6 The Scuola di San Cristoforo dei Mercanti (before restoration of the lower parts of the walls)

* This is the period of the merging
of the Scuola dei Mercanti, which
was originally at the Frari, with the
Scuola di San Cristoforo, founded at
the Madonna dell'Orto in 1377.
Palladio was paid 15 ducats in 1571
for some advice on the design of the
building.

Around 1570, the *casa* of the Scuola of San Cristoforo dei Mercanti, founded in the mid-fifteenth century,* was built next to the church (see plate 6) and was later decorated with paintings by Jacopo Tintoretto and his son Domenico, Paolo Veronese and others. When the French suppressed the *scuole* in 1806, it contained no less than ninety-two paintings, ten of which were chosen for the collections of Eugène de Beauharnais, Viceroy of Napoleon's *Regno Italico*. Several of them are now in the Accademia of Venice, including an *Annunciation* by Paolo Veronese, and the rest are now dispersed.

When in 1668 the secular canons of San Giorgio in Alga were suppressed by Pope Clement IX, the monastery and church were acquired by monks of the Cistercian order from San Tommaso di Torcello. When in their turn, they were *licenziati* (1787) the monastery was closed, and the church, administered by the priest of San Marziale as an Oratory, became the property of the Republic. In 1855 the church was also closed, and only re-opened in 1869 after a substantial restoration. It then became a Parish Church. In 1931, the charitable order of the Giuseppini, already established in the nearby Patronate of Pius IX since 1883, took over the Madonna dell'Orto and continue there today.

It perhaps seems strange that few travellers knew the Madonna dell'Orto before its recent restoration by the Italian Art and Archives Rescue Fund. Nowadays, the church receives many visitors. It is a change that would have gratified John Ruskin, who wrote his history of Venice, *St Mark's Rest*, 'for the few travellers who still care for her monuments,' and who knew the church and admired it as 'an interesting example of Renaissance Gothic, the traceries of the windows being very rich and quaint' (see plate 7) and containing 'most important Tintorettos' (*Stones of Venice*, Vol. III). But even then he observed that the largest ones were 'grievously injured by damp and neglect'. Of the *Last Judgment* he wrote: 'By Tintoret only has this unimaginable event been grappled with in its verity', and it was in fact Ruskin's effusive praise of Tintoretto's work that first recommended the church as a worthy subject of restoration (see plate 8).

The Madonna dell'Orto was not the first church to be considered for restoration by the British fund, which was set up after the flood of 4th November 1966 that shocked the world into realization of what the loss of Venice would mean. Nor was the comprehensive need for the restoration of the church's floor and walls, paintings, sculptures, decorations, *intonaco* (plasterwork), and electrical systems, solely due to the 1966 flood. As in so many Venetian churches, this flood came as a crowning blow after years of gradual destruction by humidity and pollution.

Two basic menaces to Venetian buildings have always been the humidity caused from above by the weather and the saline humidity that creeps up from below (see for example plate 6). The answer of the Republic to these was constant vigilance and a high standard of maintenance. However, when the French came in 1797 this practice was abandoned, and for this failing the

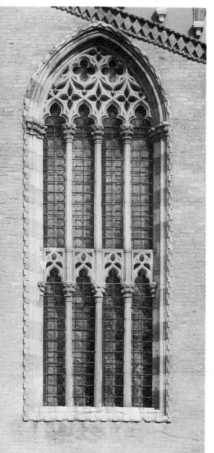

7 The façade: detail showing a window (early fifteenth century) by Giovanni and Bartolomeo Bon (?)

8 A nineteenth-century engraving of the church, and the Scuola dei Mercanti (as Ruskin saw it)

Venetians are paying a high price in terms of the increasing uninhabitability of the city.

There have been many restorations in Venice in this century, some good, some less so, but all costly. Some remarkable techniques have been developed to deal with walls, but strange to say modern damp courses were virtually unknown until the present crisis. However, it seems probable that impermeable Istrian stone, laid at the bases of the walls by the masons and architects of the Republic, was understood to constitute a kind of damp-proofing as well as a firm foundation. The only method of protecting the floor, which usually rests directly on the earth, was to build another floor on top of the old one (see plate 9).

Of the nineteenth-century restorations of the Madonna dell'Orto, the most radical was that undertaken by the Austrian authorities shortly before their occupation of Venice ended in 1866. Though first mooted in 1831, by 1845 only the façade had been restored. The church was actually closed in 1855, and used as a storehouse for wine and hay by the Austrian militia until work began in 1864 under a Viennese architect, Professor Friedrich Schmidt. The restoration, which was on Neo-Gothic lines, took five years, and involved

15

rebuilding the roof, which completely destroyed the already damaged ceiling paintings. In addition, supposed Gothic motifs were painted in and around the arches (see plate 10), the floor was relaid (necessitating the removal of the funerary inscriptions to the Chapel of San Mauro), and the façade was covered with plaster (see plate 3).

In 1912, there was some attempt to deal with the maladies to which stone is liable, and in 1930–31 there was another substantial restoration which, while rectifying some of the Neo-Gothic additions, amongst other things covered the bricks of the interior with plaster painted to resemble brick. And so we come to the restoration sponsored by the Italian Art and Archives Rescue Fund after the flood of 1966. The preliminaries took a considerable time, and it was not until 1968 that work began under the supervision of a young architect from the *Soprintendenza ai Monumenti*, Arch. Marco Bisà, whose first assignment it was. The *Soprintendenza* first decided to rebuild on traditional lines the lower part of the church which had been attacked by rising saline damp, and to insert a damp course. At the same time, the cleaning of the pictures got under way in the newly created laboratory of San

9 *Above:* A section of the church floor, showing how new floors were superimposed on the old

10 *Opposite:* The interior in 1925, showing the effects of the Austrian restoration of 1864–69. Note the painted ceiling, and the decorative motifs on the nave wall and inside the arches

* A modern replica of the Madonna dell'Orto exists in Bohemia (see plate 11). The Church of Santa Maria Immacolata at Eichwald (Duby) near Teplitz was started in 1897 and consecrated in 1906. Prince Carlos Clary von Aldringen had the church built in memory of his mother, who lived for many years in Venice and died there. The idea for building this church came to Prince Clary when he saw, pinned to the door of the Basilica of Torcello, a drawing of a lovely gothic arch which could be bought at a stonecutter's yard in Venice, and which had once been part of a church on the island of San Giorgio in Alga. He then started collecting pieces of early Gothic works in marble, to be used when the church was built. The architect was a Venetian, Prof. Pietro Bigaglia, who took the Church of the Madonna dell'Orto as his model and brought a team of Venetian artisans and workmen with him. The marble for the façade and other parts of the building came from Venice, and the bricks from Ferrara. The church in Eichwald is now kept in perfect condition by the Czechoslovak government.

Gregorio. As the Madonna dell'Orto was a pilot operation, it was urgent to start work in order to stimulate similar action elsewhere in Venice; and such it has done. Since then, there have been experiments on other buildings with other systems, such as the preservation of the ancient brickwork through consolidation, and waterproofing by chemical means. In the following pages, an attempt is made to let the photographs for the most part carry the story of the restoration.*

11 The Church of Santa Maria Immacolata, Eichwald, Bohemia. A modern replica of the Madonna dell'Orto

1 The structural restoration

Preface
by Renato Padoan

Within the boundaries chosen for their city, the Venetians, over a period of eleven hundred years, built as many as a hundred and seventy churches, large and small. In modern times, the *Soprintendenza ai Monumenti* has been the only source of help for the parish priests for urgent maintenance work to their churches. It was never possible to undertake restoration work on a large scale to combat various and grave problems such as saline humidity.

After the flood of 1966, the British *Italian Art and Archives Rescue Fund* were the first to request to undertake an exhaustive restoration of the decayed and endangered features of a church.

In the Madonna dell'Orto, rising damp had penetrated the walls to a height of twelve feet in places, affecting the plaster, brickwork, decorations, friezes and doors. The brick and stone in a wall absorb the damp which deposits harmful salts as it evaporates. As a consequence, the mortar was turning to dust and the walls breaking up. The only solution was a complete rebuilding of the lower part of the church, using the traditional techniques, and the installation simultaneously of a damp course which would prevent the damp from rising above a certain point.

This was not the only cause of humidity in the church. The vast floor, resting directly on the earth, allowed over a large area the rising of vapour into the church atmosphere. When, in spring, the air became considerably warmer than the still-cold ground, the vapour would condense on all the exposed surfaces of the building.

This problem was eliminated by isolating the floor from the damp ground, so as to shut off the rising vapour as well as to stabilize the temperatures of the floor and the air above it. As a consequence, the air is now drier and the continual deposit of chemicals on the church's works of art, left by the condensed vapour, has largely ceased.

As a result of this work and of the other restorations which are described in the following pages, the Madonna dell'Orto has been made safe, and returned to its original majestic splendour. And I wish to express my warmest thanks to Sir Ashley Clarke and the Venice in Peril Fund.

Restoring the church

12 The façade. The scaffolding went up in early summer of 1968 to enable the restoration of the decorations at the summit, and the pinnacles and niches in which the statues stand. It was also hoped at this time to clean and restore the statues themselves

13 *Above:* A pinnacle from the façade. The first disagreeable surprise when work started was that all the pinnacles in Istrian stone were in grave danger of imminent collapse. This necessitated an unforeseen, urgent and by no means easy restoration

14 *Above right:* It was necessary to carry enormous loads on aerial supports. All repairs were carried out at heights varying between 31 and 50 metres from the ground

21

15 *Above: Temperance*, from one of the pinnacles of the façade, (eighteenth century). The admirable statues of the pinnacles are almost unrecognizable because of the advanced state of sulphation

16 *Above right:* The iron clamps and braces affixed by the restorers of 1912 were capable of raising loads of several tons by centimetres owing to the difference in coefficient of expansion and an increase in volume due to oxidization. All the original parts of the stonework were re-used after consolidation and the necessary plugging

17 The north wall of the church. The lower parts of the walls all around the church were completely rebuilt, being totally and irremediably impregnated with salt and damp. A lead damp course was everywhere inserted, consisting of a layer of lead at a height about two feet from the pavement, protected above and below by layers of bitumen

18 Detail of an unrestored outside wall. Corrosive salt, deposited by rising damp, is visible on the brickwork

19 *Right:* The traditional Venetian technique for rebuilding the lower part of a wall is known as *scuci-cuci* – meaning unsew-sew. Firstly, two sections of the wall are destroyed, leaving part of the old wall isolated between. This part supports the wall above while the gaps to its left and right are rebuilt with new brick and mortar, until the rebuilt sections are once again capable of supporting the wall

20 *Below:* The next stage is to destroy the remaining section of the old wall. This part can then be rebuilt and integrated with the new to the left and right. Thus, *scuci-cuci* refers to the way in which the new wall seems to be woven into the old, replacing at intervals the corroded brick. The arrow points to the lead damp course which was installed at the same time

21 Cross-section of the church.
Drawing by Marco Bisà

The roof was reported sound. Also
the campanile, which was originally
built in 1503. A very violent storm
towards 1840 destroyed the upper
part of it and a major restoration
was effected probably
contemporaneously with the
restoration of the church itself
between 1864 and 1869. On these
no work was done in 1968–69. On
the other hand the frames of all the
upper windows were renewed and
at a later stage those of some of the
chapel windows at ground level
also

22 *Opposite:* The cloister, before restoration. The cloister of the Madonna dell'Orto was alienated from the church in 1817, and belongs now to a private individual, a boat-builder. It adjoined his workshop and was used as a deposit for the odds and ends of his trade. On two sides the roofs were in ruins; but the Gothic arches were intact. We re-opened the door leading from the cloister and allowed it to be known to the owner, a man of over eighty years of age, that if he were willing to give back the cloister to the church, our Fund would restore it with the rest of the church. No reaction

23 *Above:* The South wall and cloister. We then prevailed on the *Parroco* (the Parish Priest) to represent to him the spiritual advantages of reconciling himself with Heaven by making so generous a gift to the Church. Still no reaction. So we undertook the restoring of the south wall. We mended the arch at the end of that side of the cloister, and lightly bricked up again the door into the church

24 The cloister and south wall after restoration. One day we noticed that the junk had disappeared, the grass had been cut and one of the roofs had been repaired by the boat-builder. Two months later the roof over the south wall had also been repaired and this lovely fifteenth-century cloister could be seen again very much as it must have been when the secular Canons of St George lived in the Monastery behind

25 The north side of the cloister,
after restoration

26 The south aisle, during
restoration, showing the cloister
door re-bricked

27 *Above right:* Looking towards the Tintoretto chapel. The lower part of the wall has been completely rebuilt; the old *intonaco* (plaster) has been removed and walls await the new. Note the largely plaster figure of the *Madonna dell'Orto*, later removed to the Chapel of San Mauro, through the door on the right

28 *Right:* The same, after the application of the fresh *intonaco* which was coloured white with a tinge of yellow

29 *Opposite above:* Restoring the floor. The original estimate of restoration work required in the church did not include any operation on the floor. But as the work advanced, it became clear that the floor was one of the chief causes of damp and condensation. It became necessary to take up completely the floor of the nave (and subsequently of the side-aisles) and reconstruct it with the object of (1) stopping the continual washing away of earth through the rise and fall of the tides, which had caused cavities under the floor. This had dangerous consequences for the floor itself and for the altars standing on it; (2) preventing excessive falls in the temperature of the marble surfaces. A sharp difference between the cold floor and the warm humid air resulted in condensation on all the interior surfaces

30 *Opposite below:* The problem was complicated by the discovery of an earlier floor in red and yellow terracotta, destroyed in 1864 to make way for a new floor in slabs of red and yellow marble. Below both of these was an even earlier floor in Venetian *terrazza*, which consisted of crushed terracotta, stone and marble fragments laid in cement

31 *Above:* After some consideration as to whether to try to rebuild the floor at one of the lower levels, it was decided eventually to remake the floor at the existing level using 80 per cent of the existing slabs. This was for several reasons: the present levels of *acqua alta* (flood-tide) do not permit a lowering of the floor level; in addition, the existing floor seemed in the right relationship to the architecture of the church; and finally, considerations of economy favoured the preservation of the existing floor

The restoration was begun by digging down some 45 centimetres and then spreading gravel which was calculated to distribute rising water evenly. This was covered with a layer of ordinary concrete, and then with a layer of insulating vermiculite, on top of which the marble slabs were relaid. When the side-aisles were similarly treated, the upper concrete layer was covered with a membrane of waterproof resin

32 *Opposite:* The Valier Chapel in 1925. This chapel, the first in the left nave, was completed in 1526 in memory of Vincenzo Valier who died in 1520. It was designed and built by the brothers Andrea and Antonio Buora who also built the Cloister of the Bay Trees of the Church of San Giorgio Maggiore. The altar originally displayed the painting of *St Vincent Deacon and four Saints* by Palma il Vecchio which is now on the wall of the neighbouring chapel. The elegant architecture, with its small cupola, is early Renaissance in character, but much disguised by its dilapidated state and by the addition of a flat wall which cuts off the original semi-circular apse. The purpose may have been to make the chapel a baptistry with adjoining vestry

33 *Above:* The Valier Chapel after its restoration of 1932. The painting on the altar is the *Madonna and Child* by Giovanni Bellini, which had been placed here for the first time in 1869

34 *Above:* Right wall of the Valier Chapel. 1969. The wall was so deeply impregnated by salt humidity that it was decided to rebuild it entirely, installing the damp-course at the same time

35 *Right:* Apse of the Valier Chapel, during restoration. It was decided to remove the wall behind the altar and restore the chapel to its original state. This involved rebuilding the right side of the arch

36 *Opposite:* The Valier Chapel, after restoration. The semi-circular apse is now exposed, and the freshly plastered walls articulate the simple features of the architecture

37 *Below:* The old high altar. All the altars in the church needed some degree of restoration, largely on account of the inadequate foundations. The high altar did not appear to date back further than the 1864 restoration. When it was dismantled, it was found to contain a monolithic slab of Istrian stone measuring some five metres in length and weighing several hundredweight. There can be little doubt that this was the original altar

38 *Opposite:* The interior of the church after restoration. The pictures have been returned and the *intonaco* (plasterwork) gives a fresh appearance to the walls. The altar can be seen in its new simplified form

Electricity, lighting and heating

The electrical system was completely renovated on orthodox lines. This in itself was advantageous and should have led to a satisfactory illumination of the church. Unfortunately this was not to be.

Appropriate illumination of ancient buildings and their contents is clearly one of the most difficult things to achieve anywhere. In Venice, it would be difficult to point to any single church where, by modern standards, it has been successfully installed.

A church requires three forms of lighting: (1) a work-a-day provision for the use of a minor altar or the cleaning of a side-chapel; (2) a normal Sunday illumination which will permit the reading of the Breviary or Prayer book; and (3) a festive illumination of the artistic treasures of the building and provision for the art historian, sightseer, student, etc. Provision for (1) is obviously not difficult; (2) depends very much on the proportions of the church, especially the height. The really difficult problem is (3).

At the Madonna dell'Orto, the *Soprintendenza ai Monumenti* rejected the practical but rather modest system proposed by Mr Anthony Swain in favour of placing the lights for (2) in the very high ceiling, and adopting an elaborate adjustable system for illuminating certain of the paintings. We can only hope that whoever next restores the church will be able to improve on this.

The heating was a set-back for a different reason. The compelling need to restore the floor caused us to throw in resources earlier earmarked for heating. The purpose of the heating was not primarily to make worship more comfortable, but to maintain as far as possible an even temperature and thus obviate condensation – one of the most insidious dangers to marble. The premature ending of our resources compelled us to leave to the Italian State the installation of effective but silent heating apparatus at some later date.

11 The sculpture

Preface

When the Church of the Madonna dell'Orto was founded in the middle of the fourteenth century by Fra Tiberio da Parma, it was first dedicated to St Christopher. Around 1460, when the decoration of the façade was being completed it was decided to place a statue of St Christopher over the main portal (see page 10). It is generally agreed that the work was entrusted to Bartolomeo Bon, a member of the nearby Scuola dei Mercanti, already famed for his decorations (in collaboration with his father Giovanni Bon) of the Cà d'Oro and the Porta della Carta of the Doge's Palace. Bon died in 1464, and so the *St Christopher* represents a late, and arguably the finest of his sculptural works. In 1969, it was the subject of one of the most striking and successful of all the restorations in the Madonna dell'Orto, but before beginning the project it was necessary to solve a difficult problem of aesthetics, and overcome the doubts of those who think that sculpture should not be cleaned or restored as paintings are.

Like everything in nature, stone is vulnerable to weathering and ageing, which alters or mellows its original appearance. In particular, it can develop a crust created by the absorption of pollutants from the air which leave chemical deposits on the surfaces. This encrustation in some degree protects the stone; and in building façades and sculpture is often much admired for the way it softens the harsh appearance of freshly cut stone. As a consequence, the cleaning of stone has been regarded by many as the desecration of the beauty of timeworn objects. It is because of this point of view that the science of stone restoration has only developed in recent years. When we sought the permission of the *Soprintendenza ai Monumenti* to undertake the cleaning of *St Christopher* we came up against the – perfectly understandable – reluctance to authorize what seemed like the destruction of the natural ageing of the work.

However, the case is altered in two respects. Firstly, the quantity of hostile chemicals in the atmosphere has increased considerably in this century, and accelerated damaging processes which affect the stone. The effects of pollution are of course not natural but man-made. Secondly, the stone of which *St Christopher* is carved is not porous like some marbles, which develop a skin formed of chemicals deposited by the passage of water. Istrian stone is extremely compact and resistant. It comes from the Istrian peninsula (now Yugoslavia) and, in the days of the Republic, was by far the most preferred building material because of its relative durability. The ageing process to which it is subject far from enhances the sculpture – rather it severely disfigures it. The head of *Faith* (see plate 39), a figure from the topmost pinnacle of the façade, is typical of what happens. Not only does *she* appear blind, but, because the sooty incrustation, which is caused by the action of sulphur in the air, disguises the details of the head and drapery, the spectator too is blinded to the character or quality of the sculpture. The more grave fact is that this blotchy black and white appearance is due not to the accumulation of harmless chemicals on the outside of the stone, but to the actual erosion and transformation of the stone itself. This was discovered and analysed for the first time by Kenneth Hempel during preliminary studies of the *St Christopher*.

Confronted with the destructive nature of the ageing of Istrian stone, permission was readily given for *St Christopher* to be restored. Had our resources been inexhaustible, we might have cleaned and consolidated the remaining twenty figures of the façade.

The restoration of *St Christopher* was undertaken by Signorina Giulia Musumeci after initial training at the Victoria and Albert Museum, under the guidance of Mr Kenneth Hempel of the Conservation Department of that museum.

39 *Opposite:* The head of *Faith*, one of the pinnacle statues from the façade, unrestored, showing the disfiguring effects of atmospheric corrosion

The cleaning
of St Christopher

by Kenneth Hempel

Of the sculptural figures that adorn the façade of the Madonna dell'Orto, the most significant is the figure of *St Christopher* standing as guardian and patron over the doorway of the church. Though boldly carved, this fine sculpture was difficult to view because it was so camouflaged with corrosion (see plate 40). Its condition and pre-eminence marked it down as a suitable subject to herald a programme of sculpture restoration in Venice. Great care and thought had to be exercised, as it was to be the first carved Istrian stone to be cleaned in the city.

The contrast in black and white exhibited by the statue before restoration requires explanation. Istrian stone is composed mainly of two compounds: calcium carbonate and magnesium carbonate. Minute samples from the blackened surface of the statue revealed, upon analysis, a corrosive layer composed of calcium sulphate loaded with carbon (soot) particles (see plate 41). All evidence points to air pollution as the cause.

Analysis of the white surface of the statue determined that magnesium carbonate had disappeared (see plate 42). The explanation of this is that magnesium carbonate is the more soluble of the two components, and dissolves with prolonged exposure to water. In general therefore, the stone turns white where the rain continually washes it, but turns black in places where the stone is sheltered (see plate 40). The widely held theory that the black corrosion protects the stone is only partly true. For a while it serves to arrest decomposition; but eventually it shells off, leaving an irregular and distorted surface. This is because the corroded layer is dissimilar in physical nature to its host. Its formation creates surface stresses because of its volume change, and this, together with its unequal reactions to changes in temperature, eventually results in scaling.

The decision to clean was taken with the realization that the restoration would not eliminate future corrosion, but would ease the existing state of corruption and, most important, facilitate future treatment aimed at lasting protection.

First the black layer was softened, and to a small extent washed away, by subjecting it to a fine spray of water for two or three days. Then, centimetre by centimetre, the remaining corrosion was removed by an ultra-sonic dental tool (see plate 43). In skilled hands this tool can distinguish between two dissimilar layers of material. The tool emits a series of minute vibrations through a cushion of water, and these are absorbed by the surface at different rates depending on the specific gravity. In this way the tool need never touch the underlying uncorroded stone (see plate 44). As the black crust disintegrated the true appearance of the stone was revealed. Not only did the form become legible but details emerged that were hidden (see plates 45–46).

The right arm was found to have been carved from a separate piece of stone (see plate 47). This was probably contrived to allow for stresses occurring from the iron staff. It had been clamped and mortared into place, but both clamps and mortar had perished. It was felt that to retain the iron staff constituted an added burden on the ageing stone, and finally a teak one was substituted. The arm was removed, cleaned and refitted with stainless steel clamps, and mortared into position with Araldite AY 103, glass sand and titanium white pigment (see plate 48).

Does cleaning by itself serve any purpose? The protection and consolidation of stone as compact as Istrian stone present problems which have still not been definitively solved. However, the operation showed that protection of the stone against future corrosion should only be carried out after a cleaning of the kind to which St Christopher was subjected.

St Christopher is still patron and protector of the church. When he was led to his martyrdom on the Island of Samos in AD 250 under the Emperor Decius, he prayed that all who saw him and trusted in God might be saved from Fire, Storm and Earthquake. Had pollution been the universal threat it is today, these photographs, taken before and after restoration, suggest that he would have included it in the list (see plates 49–51).

40 *Left: St Christopher and Child* attributed to Bartolomeo Bon, *c.* 1460, before restoration

41 A particle, magnified 19 times, showing the corroded black crust from *St Christopher*, consisting of calcium sulphate and carbon (soot)

42 A similar particle taken from the white surface of *St Christopher*. Arrows point to the bleached surface, which has lost magnesium carbonate

43 The ultra-sonic dental tool used for the cleaning of *St Christopher*

44 The ultra-sonic dental tool in use

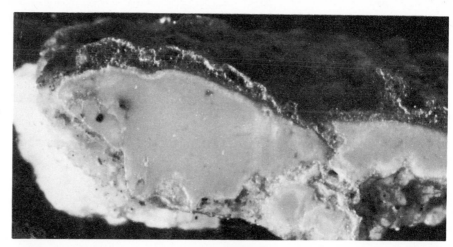

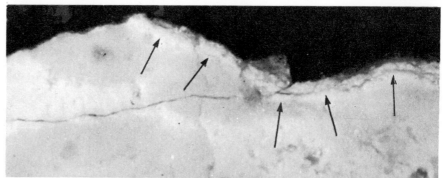

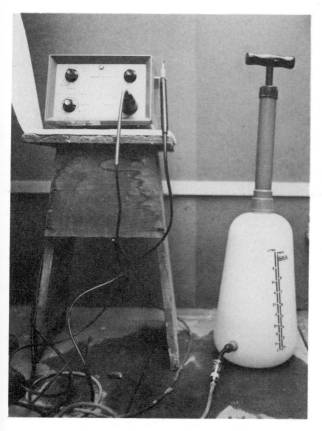

45 *Right:* The medallion of *St Christopher's* cloak, before restoration

46 *Below:* The medallion of *St Christopher's* cloak, after restoration

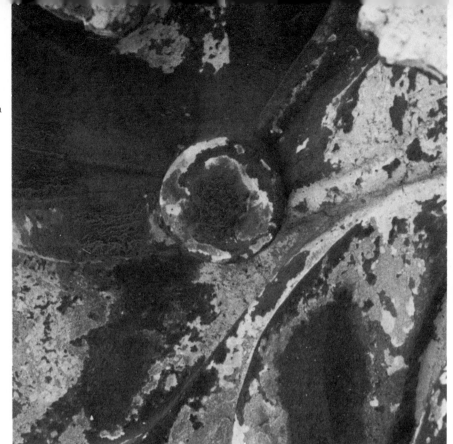

47 *Right: St Christopher's* right
arm, before restoration

48 *Below right: St Christopher's*
right arm, after restoration

49 *Above: St Christopher's* head,
before restoration

50 *Right: St Christopher's* head,
after restoration

51 *Opposite: St Christopher and
Child*, attributed to Bartolomeo
Bon, after restoration

52 *The Adoration of the Golden Calf,*
before restoration

III The paintings

The Laboratory of San Gregorio and the restoration of the paintings

by Francesco Valcanover

The restoration of Jacopo Tintoretto's paintings put to the test the abilities of the restoration laboratory of San Gregorio and its scientific and documentation departments. These had been established in 1968 in the former church of San Gregorio and in an adjacent building, both of which had been placed at the disposal of the *Soprintendenza alle Gallerie ed Opere d'Arte* by the *Comune* of Venice.

The creation of this laboratory had been planned for some time, but it became a reality only after the exceptionally high flood of 4th November 1966, which vividly emphasized the seriousness of the decay threatening Venice's unique artistic heritage. The *Soprintendenza ai Monumenti*, with funds conceded by the *Direzione Generale delle Antichità e Belle Arti*, undertook the radical restoration of the fifteenth century church, while the *Soprintendenza alle Gallerie* provided for the utilities (heating, light, water, and gas).

Contributions by private rescue committees and funds played an essential part in founding the restoration laboratory. Through the intervention of the Ambassador of West Germany in Rome, Hans H. Herwarth von Bittenfeld, eighteen modern lighting complexes were provided by the Germans; the American Committee to Rescue Italian Art placed on deposit apparatus for photography and special rays; the Dutch *Comité Geteisterde Kunsteden Italie* and the British committee of *Italia Nostra* gave instruments for scientific research. However, the most substantial assistance was given by the Italian Art and Archives Rescue Fund. Under the enlightened chairmanship of Sir Ashley Clarke, the Fund gave equipment for the restoration laboratory, and entrusted to Miss Joyce Plesters, of the National Gallery, London, the planning of the scientific department. The Fund gave the most urgently needed instruments for this department, arranged for practical instruction in their use, and undertook to pay a chemical assistant and photographer for three years.

The new restoration complex allowed the immediate realization of a policy whereby the *Soprintendenza alle Gallerie* would co-operate with the *Soprintendenza ai Monumenti* in the simultaneous restoration of both architectural monuments and the cultural treasures preserved in them. The first fruit of this policy was the restoration of the Madonna dell'Orto. The radical treatment of the church itself, supervised by the *Soprintendenza ai Monumenti* and financed by the Italian Art and Archives Rescue Fund, was accompanied by the treatment of Tintoretto's paintings, which the

Soprintendenza alle Gallerie entrusted to Antonio Lazzarin and his team, assisted by State funds.

Firstly it was necessary to solve the difficult technical problems of the removal and transportation to San Gregorio of the two largest paintings (see plates 53, 54, 57). Next, the state of preservation of the eleven canvases was carefully documented. Fragments of paint and of the ground, X-ray photographs and the study of the paintings under special lights, indicated the extent of paint loss, of repaintings, and of the disturbing effects of a thick layer of non-original varnishes. Furthermore, the close examination revealed immediately and definitively that one of the five *Virtues* – the *Faith* – from the vaults of the apse (see plate 100) did not belong to the catalogue of paintings by Tintoretto, or even his workshop. It is clearly a seventeenth century work, recorded for the first time in 1733 above the west door of the church.

The task of restretching the canvases was begun with the detachment of the lining canvases and the removal of the decomposed glue. The exposure of the original supports showed that Tintoretto had used canvas of widely divergent qualities for the *Last Judgment* and the *Adoration of the Golden Calf* (see plates 92, 93). It also revealed the exact extent of some later additions to the *Last Judgment*, among which were the seventeenth-century heads of a man and a woman, most probably copies of donor's portraits made when the originals were taken to adorn the family *palazzo*. Of all the pictures, the relinings of the *Last Judgment* and the *Adoration of the Golden Calf* were naturally the most arduous, since Tintoretto has used a large number of canvases stitched together. During restoration they withstood the careful removal of the stitching, after fine gauze had been applied as reinforcement along the seams.

Once the surface of the paintings had been consolidated by the adhesion of the new lining to the original support, the cleaning could begin. The best preserved canvases were the *St Agnes reviving Licinio* and the former organ doors representing the *Presentation of the Virgin in the Temple*, the *Vision of the Cross to St Peter*, and the *Beheading of St Paul*. The original paint surface of the *Vision of the Cross to St Peter* was almost completely intact, and the *Presention of the Virgin* and the *Beheading of St Paul* had minor abrasions of the surface which far from justified the heavy eighteenth-century repainting of the backgrounds. The *St Agnes reviving Licinio* benefited considerably from the elimination of a thick and much-yellowed varnish. This had been applied during a restoration in the early nineteenth century, when the picture was taken to Paris, and it had been left intact during a cleaning at the time of the Tintoretto exhibition in Venice in 1937. The rediscovered liveliness of its colours affirms a dating towards the end of the 1560s, and the cleaning also revealed the intervention of assistants from the workshop.

No serious paint loss was suffered by the *Adoration of the Golden Calf*, even in the clouds which separate Moses from the Worship of the Golden Calf. These had been unaccountably repainted and the cleaning exposed the original paint in good condition underneath. On the other hand, there are

54

extensive and numerous *lacunae* in the *Last Judgment*; in particular, in the lower left corner, loss of paint was almost complete and even the support had been replaced, which argued against the removal of the nineteenth-century repainting.

The same compromise appears under the repaintings and the thick layer of non-original and discoloured varnishes of Tintoretto's four *Virtues* – *Justice*, *Strength*, *Temperance*, and *Prudence* – and the fifth, by an anonymous painter of the seventeenth century, depicting *Faith*. The paint loss was concentrated in the robes and backgrounds and the gaps were filled by matching tempera colours (see plates 94–100).

The recent restoration, beyond halting a process of decay which had occasioned serious damage, presented an opportunity for evaluating the place of these works in Tintoretto's *oeuvre*.

As Coletti has already suggested in his monograph on Tintoretto of 1940, the *Presentation of the Virgin* can be placed between 1552 and 1553 by virtue of his interest in complex figure groups in a confined perspective setting: an interest apparent in other works of the early 1550s. No less convincing is the year 1556, again proposed by Coletti, for the *Vision of the Cross to St Peter* and the *Beheading of St Paul*. This is the date of the final payment for the doors of the Madonna dell'Orto's lost organ. The vivid, almost tangible, brilliance of the colours reflects the influence of Paolo Veronese, who for a brief spell in the mid-1550s captivated Tintoretto.

The restoration has also made it possible to date the two large canvases of the choir. Only now in fact can suggestions by some critics that these belong to the early 1560s be confirmed. They recognized in these works Tintoretto's desire to express the visionary element of religious mysteries. He achieved this by subduing bright colours and by pervading the scene with a glowing light; a manner which attained its climax in his cycle of paintings for the Scuola di San Rocco, Venice.

The four *Virtues* are of the same date as the two choir paintings. Since restoration, these also throw a new light on Tintoretto's activity. They seem to anticipate, in their sinuous elegance (which is an echo of the figure style of the Mannerists), the *Philosophers* of the Marcian Library.

Naturally, in time to come, it will be possible to evaluate fully the outcome of the restoration of Tintoretto's paintings in the Madonna dell'Orto. Meanwhile, however, it represents one of the most outstanding episodes of the intense activity of conservation and preservation of Venice's cultural patrimony in the years following the flood of 4th November 1966.

Restoring the Tintorettos

by Francesco
Valcanover

53 *Above right:* Tintoretto's *Last Judgment* is lowered from the wall of the choir. This painting, and the *Adoration of the Golden Calf* are each 14.50 × 59.0 metres and their vast dimensions made it a difficult task to remove the canvases from the church. They were first removed from their stretchers, and then wrapped around a specially devised cylinder

54 *Right:* Tintoretto's *Last Judgment* is rolled on to the cylinder. The cylinder was made of light three-ply wood, and its diameter 80 centimetres was calculated in relation to the length of the canvases. The walls of the choir have been affected by rising damp, which has corroded the brickwork and bleached the plaster. There are also traces of damp in the old wooden stretcher behind the canvas

55 *Above right:* After relining and cleaning, the *Last Judgment* awaits varnishing. This vast canvas, and the *Presentation of the Virgin* on the left, give an indication of the dimensions of the former church of San Gregorio

56 *Right:* The new and immense moveable stretcher for the *Last Judgment*, secured against the columns of the church, waits while the painting itself is unrolled

57 *Above left:* The *Last Judgment* and the *Adoration of the Golden Calf*, wrapped around the 6.20 metre roller, entering the restoration laboratory of San Gregorio. The roller was mounted on two mobile supports to avoid any disturbance of the fragile pigment of the paintings

58 *Above right:* After the removal of the old lining and the thick layer of decomposed glue, the process of relining begins on the *Last Judgment*. The new lining as can be seen consists of a number of canvases sewn together

59 *Right:* This photograph, showing the *Adoration of the Golden Calf* after relining, illustrates the vast scale of Tintoretto's two paintings for the choir of the church. Lying on the floor of the Laboratory is one of the *Virtues, Strength*

60 The return of the paintings to
the choir and to the apse walls was
effected by means of scaffolding
specially designed to take the weight
of the two largest pictures,
amounting to more than one ton
each

61 The east end of the Madonna
dell'Orto, after restoration and the
return of the paintings. The
restoration of the church has
eliminated two of the main causes of
damage to the paintings: the
condensation which affected the
surface of the pictures, and the rising
damp which affected the pictures
as well as the wooden stretchers
from behind

62 *The Presentation of the Virgin in
the Temple*. Oil on canvas. 4.29 ×
4.80 metres, after restoration.
(Right side aisle.) This painting is
made up of the two external panels
of the doors of the lost organ which
was dismantled in the nineteenth
century. This used to be situated
approximately where this painting
now is

63 *Above: The Presentation of the Virgin*. Detail of the Virgin and the High Priest, under a raking light. One can see the advanced state of disintegration of the paint surface

64 *Above right: The Presentation of the Virgin*. The same detail, after the re-integration of the paint, and the removal of discolouring varnish

65 *Overleaf left: The Vision of the Cross to St Peter*. Oil on canvas. 4.20 × 2.40 metres, before restoration. (Apse of the church). This painting was originally on the inside of the left door of the organ. The trial cleaning of a small area to the right of the saint's head suggests the degree of deterioration from the original colour values. Such deterioration is caused by the discolouration of later repainting and varnishes

66 *Overleaf right: The Vision of the Cross to St Peter*. After restoration. Nineteenth-century patches, where the hinges of the organ door once were, are visible at the right top and bottom corners. After the pigment had been strengthened by relining, cleaning of the painting gave a new limpidity to the colour

67 *The Beheading of St Paul.* Oil on
Canvas. 4.30 × 2.40 metres, after
restoration. (Apse of the church).
This was painted for the inside of
the right door of the old organ

68 *Above right: The Beheading of St Paul.* Detail before restoration. The two trial areas of cleaning show the thick layer of dirt and discoloured varnish which covers the original paint. The results of some previous restorations are only too evident in the Saint's back and in the rays of light below the angel with the symbols of martyrdom

69 *Right: The Beheading of St Paul.* The same detail after restoration. The *pentimento,* showing Tintoretto's first idea for the painting of the Executioner's garment, is apparent after the cleaning (see the arrows)

70 *The Adoration of the Golden Calf.*
Oil on canvas. 14.50 × 5.90 metres,
after restoration.(Left wall of the
choir). This painting illustrates two
scenes: Moses receiving the Tablets
of Law, and the Worship of the
Golden Calf

71 *Above right: The Adoration of the Golden Calf.* Detail of the lower half, before restoration

72 *Right: The Adoration of the Golden Calf.* The same detail after restoration

73 *Right: The Adoration of the Golden Calf*, after restoration. Detail of Moses on Mount Sinai

74 *Below: The Adoration of the Golden Calf*, after restoration. Detail of the Israelites bringing jewels to the ceremony. This, and the other detail of Moses (plate 72), shows how in many places the painting has preserved its original 'glazes', which are the last and often the finest touches or films of paint to be applied, to adjust a detail or colour tone, and which are always the first to disappear if the surface of the painting is roughly treated

75 *The Last Judgment.* Oil on canvas. 14.50 × 5.90 metres, after restoration. (Right wall of the choir)

76 *Top right: The Last Judgment.*
Detail of the flood, in the middle of
the painting. A photograph taken in
1950

77 *Centre right: The Last Judgment.*
The same detail, before the
restoration of 1969. The comparison
between this and the photograph of
1950 (plate 76) demonstrates the
rapid deterioration of Tintoretto's
masterpiece. In a brief space of time,
owing to the continual worsening of
atmospheric conditions, there had
been a marked discolouration of the
varnish and retouches. Especially
striking in both figures is the crack
of the seam of the canvas which
crosses the female nude borne up by
the angels

78 *Right: The Last Judgment.* The
same detail after restoration in 1969.
This very characteristic passage of
Tintoretto's has become much
sharper in detail and more legible
since the removal of the accumulated
dirt and the varnish. In addition, the
removal of repaints in the clouds, the
pouring rain and the whirling
torrent, has revealed the complex
interplay of light and space, and the
concise rapidity of the brushwork

79 *Above right: The Last Judgment.* before restoration. Detail of the lower left corner, which was repainted in the nineteenth century. X-rays established that much of the original paint was missing in this area (see plates 86 and 87), and that the nineteenth-century paint was laid in directly on the support. It was decided therefore to leave the repainting intact and only to remove old varnishes and dirt

80 *Right: The Last Judgment.* The same detail, after restoration. It was discovered that in the lower left corner the canvas had been replaced in the nineteenth century, and this area had been marked off by a thin grey line

81 *Above right: The Last Judgment*, before restoration. Detail of two damned women from the lower left side of the canvas. The trial area of cleaning, on the falling woman's head, showed that it was sufficient to remove dirt and varnishes to restore the picture to its original condition

82 *Right: The Last Judgment.* The same detail, after restoration

83 *Top right: The Last Judgment.*
Detail of Donor's heads, before
restoration, from high up on the
right of the painting. Even before
relining, it became clear that these
heads were later additions to
Tintoretto's canvas

84 *Centre right: The Last Judgment.*
The same detail, under a raking
light. The exact extent of the
addition, which can be seen fairly
clearly in plate 83, became obvious
in this slanting light

85 *Right: The Last Judgment.* The
same detail after restoration. The
head of St Jerome can be seen on the
left

86 *Above: The Last Judgment*. Detail
of plate 79 before restoration

87 *Above right: The Last Judgment.*
X-ray photograph of the same
detail, showing the lack of
Tintoretto's own work under the
repainting

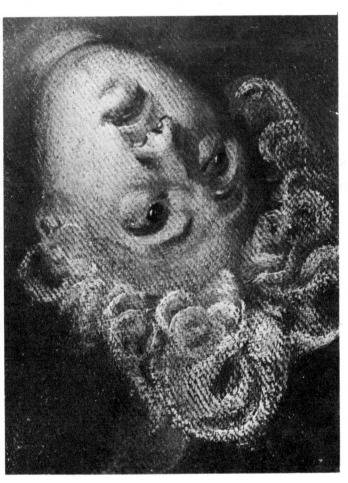 

88 *Above: The Last Judgment*. Detail
of plate 82. The brushwork in this
passage quite clearly contrasts with
that in plate 86, and is Tintoretto's
own

89 *Above right: The Last Judgment*.
An X-ray photograph of the same
detail, showing the freedom of
Tintoretto's technique

90 *Below:* Diagram showing the composition of the canvases in the *Last Judgment*

91 *Below right:* Diagram showing the composition of canvases in the *Adoration of the Golden Calf*

92 *Right: The Adoration of the Golden Calf.* Original canvas sample. Actual size

93 *Far right: Last Judgment.* Original canvas sample. Actual size

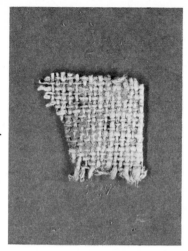

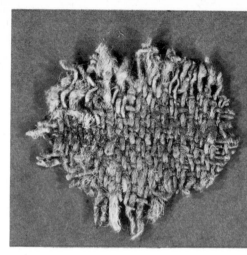

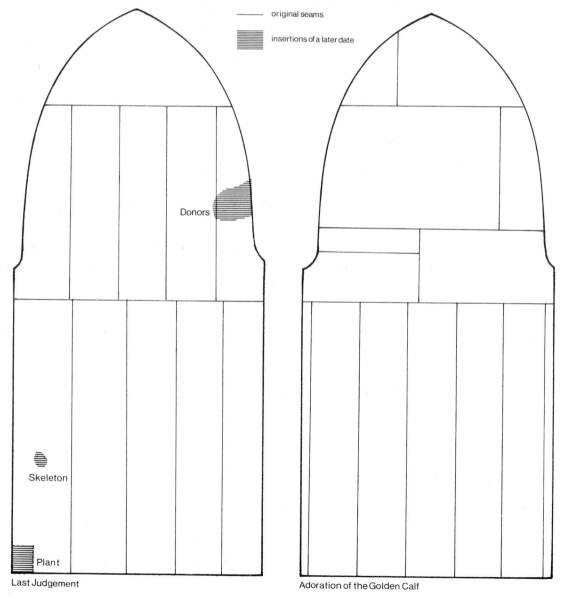

—— original seams

▤ insertions of a later date

Donors

Skeleton

Plant

Last Judgement

Adoration of the Golden Calf

94 *Top left: Justice*. Oil on canvas. 4.50 × 2.40 metres, before restoration. (Apse of the Church)

95 *Top right: Justice*, after cleaning. This, and the other *Virtues* were found to have been repainted very roughly in the past to hide serious losses of paint, which are revealed here in the cleaned painting, before restoration

96 *Left: Justice*, after restoration

97 *Right: Strength*. Oil on canvas. 4.50 × 2.40 metres, after restoration

98 *Left: Prudence*. Oil on canvas.
4.50 × 2.40 metres, after restoration

99 *Centre: Temperance*. Oil on
canvas. 4.50 × 2.40 metres, after
restoration

100 *Right: Faith*. Oil on canvas.
4.50 × 2.40 metres, after restoration.
As discovered during the
examination of this painting,
this is not by Tintoretto, but by an
unknown seventeenth-century
painter

101 *St Agnes reviving Licinio*. Oil on Panel. 4.00 × 2.00 metres, before restoration. (The Contarini Chapel, left aisle of the church)

This painting was commissioned by Tommaso Contarini for his family chapel, built about 1563, and was probably executed in the late 1560s. There are records of at least three restorations before that of 1968–69: the first was carried out in Paris where it was transferred at the Fall of the Republic; the second in Venice around 1851; and the third in 1936–37. The thick varnishes which result from these restorations had deteriorated, and rendered the interpretation of both design and colour difficult. The removal of the layer of dirt and varnish have restored this Tintoretto to its original state. This affords new clues to its date, hitherto a matter of considerable controversy

102 *St Agnes reviving Licinio*, after restoration. The painting shows St Agnes, Patron Saint of Virgins, on her way to martyrdom during Diocletian's persecutions. She is seen restoring to life the son of a Roman Prefect who was, thereby, converted to Christianity

103 *St Agnes reviving Licinio*, after
restoration. Detail of the heads of St
Agnes' Judge (*right*) and of her
attendants

The examination of the Tintorettos

by Joyce Plesters and
Lorenzo Lazzarini

Early biographers of Jacopo Tintoretto would have us believe that he was virtually self-taught, an almost unheard-of phenomenon in an age when a long and strict apprenticeship was the only mode of entry into the painter's profession. The artist's astonishing originality and diversity, not just in style but also in technique, would lend credence to their assertions, but for the fact that of a number of pictures by Tintoretto which we have been privileged to examine, it seems to be the earliest which are painted in the most traditional technique, the artist reserving his most daring experiments for his mature and later years.

One assertion by early biographers which can be confirmed is that he sought out commissions and got them through his own efforts. This is particularly true of two of his most important projects in Venice, the great canvases of the *Adoration of the Golden Calf* and *Last Judgment* in the Madonna dell'Orto (see plates 70 and 75), and the vast cycle of paintings at the Scuola di San Rocco. The first of these commissions, that at the Madonna dell'Orto, he secured by offering to do what looked like a nearly impossible task for a derisory fee – too good a bargain for the Prior of the Madonna dell'Orto to turn down.

The second he got by downright trickery. In both cases he offered to do the work for little more than the cost of the materials and his expenses. The two institutions represent two of the main attachments in his life – the Scuola di San Rocco where he expended so much of his time and energy for the glory of God, and the Madonna dell'Orto, his local church where he worshipped and where he and his family were to be buried. The works we see of his at the Madonna dell'Orto and at the Scuola di San Rocco must surely be what he wanted to paint and how he wanted to paint, and perhaps with less participation from assistants than in his official commissions at the Ducal Palace.

Tintoretto is recorded as having contracted to do work for the Madonna dell'Orto as early as 1548. This contract relates to the painting of *The Presentation of the Virgin in the Temple,* on the outside doors of the organ, but the work was not in fact carried out until 1551–52. Some technical aspects of these organ-door paintings will be touched on briefly at the end of this Note. Unfortunately no documents have been discovered to give a date for the two gigantic canvases of the *Adoration of the Golden Calf* and the *Last Judgment* which face each other across the tall narrow choir of the Madonna dell'Orto. In the past scholars have differed widely on their dating, though most present-day art historians seem to favour *c.* 1562–64.

The pictures were obviously painted as a pair for the site they still occupy. Their rather archaic-looking pointed-arch tops are dictated by the shape of the ceiling vaulting of this typically Venetian Gothic church. What first strikes the spectator is their sheer size, a dizzy 14.5 metres (almost 48 feet) in height. What inspires awe in any restorer, conservator or student of painting technique are the tremendous problems of handling paintings of these dimensions, whether in the course of their original creation or their subsequent repair and restoration.

Practically all of Tintoretto's paintings are on canvas, including all those in the Madonna dell'Orto. In the fifteenth century most of what might be termed European easel paintings (i.e. excluding murals) were done on wood panels. It was in Venice in the sixteenth century that painting on canvas began to prevail over painting on wood panel. A likely reason was that fresco paintings proved impermanent on the damp and salt-impregnated walls, yet there was at the same time the need to cover large areas of walls and ceilings with paintings, and canvas was lightweight and cheap compared with wood.

Artists' canvas, like all woven fabrics, is supplied only in certain standard widths depending on the width of the loom. We have noticed that in Venetian sixteenth-century paintings, including those of Tintoretto, the most common width is approximately one metre (exact width, as measured on the picture, varies with the degree of tension of the canvas on the stretcher). For pictures as large as the *Adoration of the Golden Calf* and the *Last Judgment* several widths of canvas have to be seamed together, and the area under the arched top would have to be cut and sewn to shape. Diagrams of the construction of the canvases of the two paintings are shown in plates 90 and 91, which also show some later insertions and repairs. Surprisingly, the canvases of the two pictures are not of the same weave. *The Adoration of the Golden Calf* has a medium-coarse, regularly-woven, plain tabby-weave canvas, while the *Last Judgment* has an exceptionally coarse, heavy, diagonal twill. Samples of each, photographed actual size, are shown in plates 92 and 93. So far as can be discovered the fibre of both is flax. The coarseness of the canvas of the *Last Judgment* caused us to speculate as to whether the fibre might be hemp (canabis sativa), for a flourishing hemp industry existed in Italy from the Middle Ages and was connected with the manufacture of sailcloth. Unfortunately, cellulose fibres when very aged are difficult to distinguish from one another, though expert opinions favour its being flax.

In 1968 when the two pictures were to be removed from the church to the studio at San Gregorio for treatment, it was found impossible to get them out and transport them without taking the canvases off their stretchers and rolling them. It seems likely that they were probably painted *in situ*. It may be that the canvases were assembled and sewn, perhaps in the studio, then taken to the church to be nailed on to already constructed wood stretchers. Above each picture there exists a hole in the ceiling of the vault through which a pulley wire can be passed from the roof space above to enable the enormous canvases to be raised and lowered when necessary (see plate 53), and this may have been the method by which they were originally installed.

In common with most painting supports, canvas requires a coat of ground or preparation to render the surface suitable for painting. Early Italian wood panel paintings seem invariably to have a coat of gesso, a white plaster-like material consisting of gypsum (calcium sulphate) bound with animal glue, which also provided a very suitable surface for gilding and tooling. When at the beginning of the sixteenth-century Venetian painters such as Giovanni Bellini and Titian began to adopt canvas as a painting support in preference to wood panel, they carried on the tradition of applying a white gesso ground though rather more thinly than was used for panels. Although we have found that Tintoretto, particularly in his later works (though even in one or two of his earlier ones, such as the organ doors mentioned above), tended to favour a dark-coloured ground or preparation for his canvases, he seems to have decided to stick to the traditional white gesso ground for both the *Adoration of the Golden Calf* and the *Last Judgment*, perhaps with the idea of achieving greater luminosity in view of the rather poorly-lit site. It would appear that the gesso was applied after the canvas had been attached to the stretchers, for the turnover of the canvas round the edges of the stretcher has no gesso coating.

Supposing we were describing the production of a fifteenth-century Venetian painting, by, say, Vivarini, Bellini or Cima, logically the next step would be the drawing of the design of the composition on the gesso ground. This itself would probably have been preceded by a number of preliminary studies on paper. Tintoretto also did a good many preliminary drawings on paper, but only a few show the complete composition of a picture. There are one or two which are recognizable as studies for the *Adoration of the Golden Calf*. Like the majority of Tintoretto's drawings on paper, those for the *Golden Calf* are of single nude male figures, and the sheet squared up ready for enlarging the design on to canvas. However, Tintoretto's mind probably worked so fast that the final painted version often differs from the preliminary drawing not just in detail but even in the fundamental stance of the figure. It is interesting to note that in the course of microscopical examination of samples from the *Adoration of the Golden Calf* we observed several instances of a line of sparsely-scattered charcoal black particles between the white gesso ground and the paint layers proper. This we deduced to represent a preliminary black underdrawing. We did not find among the rather larger number of samples taken from the *Last Judgment* a single such example, but this may not be significant, bearing in mind the size of the samples (approximately 0.5 millimetre in diameter) compared with the overall area of the painting! The absence of underdrawing from the *Last Judgment* would, though, fit in with the fact that much more in the way of working out the composition at the painting stage seems to have occurred in the *Last Judgment* than in the *Adoration of the Golden Calf*.

Proceeding from the underdrawing to the paint layer proper, we must briefly consider what paint is. Its two essential components are the *pigments*, coloured solids in powder form, and the *medium*, for example gum, glue, egg or oil, which serves to stick the particles of pigment to each other and to the surface being painted.

86

It is the pigments which impart colour to painting, and Venetian sixteenth-century painting is renowned for its colour. The reputation for colour seems to derive from the paintings of Giorgione and from those of the young Titian and Giovanni Bellini while both were working under Giorgione's influence. At this period in Venetian painting the artist sometimes incorporates in a single picture virtually every pigment he can lay his hands on. A good example is the Titian *Bacchus and Ariadne* in the National Gallery, London. What in other hands might turn into a gaudy display, achieves rich harmony in the hands of the Venetian masters. Tintoretto, and equally his contemporary, Paolo Veronese, carried on the grand tradition of Venetian colour. The *Adoration of the Golden Calf* is revealed since cleaning to be a very colourful picture like the decorations of the ceiling and frieze in the Sala dell'Albergo of the Scuola di San Rocco, painted in 1564, soon after the *Golden Calf* and the *Last Judgment*. And, indeed, Tintoretto first found fame with one of his most colourful pictures of all, the *Miracle of the Slave*, now in the Accademia Gallery. In our microscopical examination and chemical analysis of paint samples from the *Adoration of the Golden Calf* and the *Last Judgment* we have noted the occurrence of pretty well all the pigments which could have been included in the palette of an easel painter of the time, including some less common ones. In addition to the ubiquitous lead white, carbon blacks, and red, yellow and brown ochres, we identified: natural (lapis lazuli) ultramarine; azurite (a blue basic copper carbonate mineral); smalt (a powdered blue glass which owes its colour to the presence of cobalt); indigo (a vegetable dyestuff); malachite (a green copper carbonate mineral, often found in fresco, but rarely in easel painting); verdigris (green copper acetate); translucent 'copper resinate' green glazes; lead-tin yellow (a double oxide of lead and tin); orpiment and realgar (the yellow and orange forms respective of arsenic sulphide); a range of crimson and purplish lake pigments (that is, vegetable or animal dyestuffs adsorbed on insoluble white powders like aluminium hydroxide or chalk to make red pigments). Venice, of course, had long enjoyed a privileged position with regard to pigment supplies, being the port of entry for exotic imports to Europe particularly from the East. Ridolfi, Tintoretto's principal biographer, was particularly struck by the blue dress of the majestic figure of the woman pointing with her finger to the calf in the *Adoration of the Golden Calf* (see plate 52). A photomicrograph of a cross-section through the blue paint of this dress is seen in plate Ia. The blue pigment is natural ultramarine, extracted from the semi-precious stone lapis lazuli by a lengthy and laborious process. It was brought from Afghanistan (the Venetian explorer Marco Polo visited the mines there) and was as precious as gold, so that it was often stipulated in the contract for a painting that the patron should supply it or pay separately for it. In the sample from the dress in the *Adoration of the Golden Calf* the large ultramarine particles are mixed with lead whites, not to cheapen the pigment, but to make it a brighter and more radiant blue. In a sample from a comparable blue drapery in the *Last Judgment* two ultramarine blue layers can be seen, the lower, in which the pigment is mixed with a little white to make it opaque, and the upper in which the translucent dark blue pigment is used as a glaze to give a more sombre, even richer, effect. In some of Tintoretto's paintings, for example some of the later ones in the Scuola di San Rocco, ultramarine is used sparingly or not at all. He seems to have used it lavishly on occasions when he particularly wanted to make an impression, for example in the central oval, *San Rocco in Glory*, in the Sala dell'Albergo of the Scuola di San Rocco, which won the competition enabling him to gain the commission for the decoration of the whole building, and here in the Madonna dell'Orto where he seems determined to make the biggest impression of all. The yellow and orange arsenic sulphide pigments, orpiment and realgar, are comparatively rarely found in European easel paintings except in sixteenth-century Venetian ones where the vibrant yellow of orpiment drapery, deepened in the shadows with orange realgar, may be traced through the paintings of Giorgione and Titian to Tintoretto. It was probably imported from Hungary. An example is seen in the photomicrograph (see plate Ib) of a paint cross-section from a yellow robe in the *Adoration of the Golden Calf*. Not for nothing is it called 'orpiment', that is, 'gold pigment', for the crystalline particles have a golden metallic sheen. The exceptionally wide range of hues of crimson to purple lake pigments, used by Tintoretto, which were made from animal and plant dyestuffs such as madder, brazilwood, and lac and kermes insects, and the dark blue pigment indigo are by-products of the cloth-dyeing industry. This reminds us that Tintoretto's father was a cloth dyer. The artist's real name was Jacopo Robusti, and the name by which he achieved fame, 'Tintoretto', means 'the little dyer'. In addition many of his fellow brethren of the Scuola di San Rocco were engaged in the Venetian textile and dyeing industry, so that he may have been particularly well-placed for getting supplies of these sorts of pigments.

The medium used by the sixteenth-century Venetian painters has been the source of endless speculation. The most unlikely concoctions have been passed off as the 'Venetian Secret' claiming to enable any artist to paint like a Titian or a Tintoretto, Vasari's description of many Venetian paintings of the period as being 'in oil' presumably being regarded as too simple to be true. A few small samples of paint from different coloured areas of the *Adoration of the Golden Calf* and the *Last Judgment* together with samples from some other paintings by Tintoretto, were analysed for medium in the Scientific Department of the National Gallery, London, using a modern instrumental technique, gas chromatography. The method provides accurate results from a sample of paint representing less than a square millimetre of picture surface. Not only was it ascertained that in all cases was the medium a drying oil, but that, in all but one sample, it was specifically linseed oil. The one sample to which a little doubt attached was that of white paint from the *Adoration of the Golden Calf*, which might have been walnut oil rather than linseed, or perhaps a mixture of the two. This would accord well with the fact that in contemporary documentary sources on painting techniques walnut oil is sometimes recommended for blue or white pigments in preference to linseed oil because it was considered to yellow less. Since cleaning it is noticeable that the *Golden Calf* has a rather lighter and brighter tonality than the *Last Judgment* and this was presumably intended by Tintoretto. Alas, even by modern methods of analysis, it is still not possible to discover how the oil was prepared or to detect minor additives.

88

It is, though, in the building up or layer structure of his paintings that Tintoretto displays to the full his ingenuity and originality. Here again differences show up between the pair of pictures. The *Last Judgment* is much more thickly painted and in a more complex sequence of layers than the *Adoration of the Golden Calf.* There is a convenient method for studying the layer structure of paintings under the microscope. A minute sample of paint, about 0.5 millimetre in diameter – smaller, in fact, than the proverbial pin's head – is removed from the picture, preferably from an area of existing damage or loss. It is then embedded in a block of transparent plastic and one edge of the block is ground down until the edge of the paint flake is seen. After this surface has been polished flat it can be focused under the microscope when all the sequence of layers can be seen in cross-section. Four examples of paint cross-sections from the Madonna dell'Orto pictures are shown in the colour photomicrographs (plates Ia and b and IIa and b). The maximum total thickness of paint plus ground found in *The Adoration of the Golden Calf* was about 200μ (1μ — 0.001 millimetre), whereas in the *Last Judgment* it was about 800μ, i.e. four times as thick, of which a correspondingly smaller proportion would be the gesso ground, which is quite thin, as can be seen from the cross-sections. Unfortunately in the case of the two samples from the *Adoration of the Golden Calf* of which the sections are shown, the gesso ground became detached after the sample was taken and so does not appear in the photographs of the sections. This tendency which the picture showed for the paint layers to detach from the gesso ground will have been corrected by the lining treatment received during the recent restoration.

In order to understand the unconventionality of Tintoretto's method of painting it is necessary to go back and describe the further stages of the painting of a typical fifteenth-century Italian painting. After the composition had been drawn, generally in black, on the white gesso ground, and perhaps some modelling in dark washes and white highlights done at this stage, the local colours will be laid in, say blue for the Virgin's robe, pink for the flesh, green for a tree, etc. Since the composition was already drawn and often modelled in detail before the local colouring was added there was little scope for improvisation or change and in any case the lay-out of the composition would have been restricted by the iconography of the subject. The need for more than one layer of paint would arise because the colour of a particular area needed modifying, for example the dark shadows of a vermilion robe would be produced by adding a translucent crimson glaze on top and the highlights perhaps by scumbling with a mixture of red and white. A purple colour could be produced by a crimson glaze painted over blue. This system also occurs a great deal in Tintoretto's paintings, for example in the paint section of the blue robe from the *Last Judgment* (see plate IIa), a deep blue glaze is added over an opaque blue layer. In fifteenth-century paintings the layers tend to be thin, flat and regular and applied in orderly sequence. In Tintoretto's paintings a lot more goes on which is not so orderly. Although, as has been mentioned above, the *Adoration of the Golden Calf* is thinly painted and with few layers compared with the *Last Judgment*, it still shows some typical eccentricities of Tintoretto's technique. It was remarked earlier that there is often a great difference between Tintoretto's preparatory sketches for figures and their final version in a painting, but between these two stages there is often a good deal of exploration and experiment. Tintoretto seems to go on modifying his compositions as he paints, and he seems to do this generally by drawing with the brush. In the X-radiographs of some of his paintings there can be seen to exist beneath the paint surface swirling and spiralling outlines representing *pentimenti*, changes of mind on the part of the artist. These show up on the X-radiograph when they are painted in lead white which is opaque to X-rays, but another pigment which he frequently uses for this intermediate drawing is his favourite red lake, which does not show up on X-radiographs. It can be seen, though, in paint cross-sections, often sandwiched between two opaque paint layers so that it is imperceptible on the surface of the picture. An example is shown in the paint cross-section from the yellow robe in *The Adoration of the Golden Calf* (see plate Ib), where a thin crimson line runs beneath the thick orpiment yellow paint layer.

In our experience of looking at the layer structure of a good many pictures, the *Last Judgment* is unique in its complexity. A paint cross-section such as that from the blue robe (see plate IIa) can be interpreted, however, if we assume that the artist, instead of laying in individual areas of colour on the gesso ground (as in the description above of a fifteenth-century picture), thickly painted the whole of the landscape (the mixed grey-green and brown layers), then painted the flesh of the figures on top, finally adding the drapery. In fact, Ridolfi describes how Tintoretto painted his figures nude then added drapery on top (though this has not been found to be the case in other pictures of his we have examined). This system would build up a considerable total thickness of paint layers. It would also have the advantage of speedier execution, which must have been important to Tintoretto in view of his numerous commitments and the sheer area of canvas he had to cover. Another unusual feature is to be seen in the paint layers of the landscape in the two cross-sections from the *Last Judgment*, that is the extraordinary mixture of different coloured pigment particles. In general painters of this period and earlier rarely mix more than two different pigments together (unless one pigment is white) in a single paint layer. One last and very tentative comment might be made on the *Last Judgment*. The obvious influence of Michelangelo's fresco of the same subject in the Sistine Chapel in the Vatican, which was completed in 1541, has often been produced as evidence that Tintoretto must have visited Rome to see the fresco. There is no documentary evidence for such a visit and in fact the only record of Tintoretto having travelled outside the environs of Venice is that of a journey to Mantua when he was already in his fifties. Technically there seems nothing to link Tintoretto's *Last Judgment* with Michelangelo's. The colour gamut, range of pigments, layer structure, medium and paint surface (very much that of an oil painting) and the general *modus operandi* seem totally unrelated to fresco painting in general and Michelangelo's *Last Judgment* in particular. What Tintoretto has borrowed from Michelangelo's version is the idea of the composition and this, as A. Pallucchini has recently pointed out, could have been got from the various engravings of Michelangelo's *Last Judgment* which were circulating in Venice from the 1540s onwards.

Unfortunately in the rather stressful period following the flood of 1966 when the church of the Madonna dell'Orto and its pictures were undergoing urgent restoration, time did not permit a technical study of all the paintings in the church. However, a limited examination was made of the three pictures which originally formed the doors for the organ. *The Presentation of the Virgin in the Temple* (see plate 61) was originally in two halves forming the outside of the doors, while the *Vision of the Cross to S. Peter* and the *Beheading of S. Paul* (see plates 64 and 66) were on the inside. The organ to which they belonged was lost and since then the two halves of the *Presentation* have been joined together to form a single picture and the three pictures are no longer hung together. All three differed from the *Golden Calf* and the *Last Judgment* in having, on top of a thin scraping of gesso ground, a second black ground or priming. These dark grounds are common in Tintoretto's later paintings, for example those in the Lower Hall at the Scuola di San Rocco. They are rarer, though not unknown, in his earlier works; for example a *Christ Washing His Disciples' Feet*, formerly in the church of San Trovaso in Venice and now in the National Gallery, London, has identical ground layers to the organ door canvases and there is some evidence for dating it soon after 1556, the year when the final payment for the organ shutters was made to Tintoretto, and perhaps when the paintings on the insides of the doors were finished. A dark ground, unless totally concealed by a thick opaque paint layer (as is the case with the *Peter* and *Paul* canvases from the interior of the doors), tends to impart a rather sombre all-over tone to the painting. The effect may increase as the oil paint becomes more transparent with age, or if the paint surface becomes worn by abrasion. Compared with, say, the *Adoration of the Golden Calf* the *Presentation of the Virgin* is a sombre picture, but it is lit with brilliant yellow and orange flashes of drapery in the artist's favourite orpiment and realgar pigments, and the radiance of the light at the summit of the stairs remains undimmed (some of the paintings in the Scuola di San Rocco which are thinly and sketchily painted on dark grounds have survived less well). The *Presentation of the Virgin in the Temple* inevitably invites comparison with Titian's larger version of the same subject, painted about twenty years earlier for the Scuola della Carità, now the Accademia Gallery, where it still is. It also reminds one of the rivalry which must have existed between these two giants of Venetian painting, and one cannot help thinking that Tintoretto was consciously trying to outdo Titian in his own version of the subject. A brilliant, almost flamboyant, technical trick with which Tintoretto scores is to use gold leaf for the mosaic pattern of the risers of the steps, leading the spectator's eye upwards. This was a bold thing to do at a time when most painters had just abandoned the use of metallic gold, even for haloes. Yet it comes off splendidly and also calls to mind the fact that Tintoretto did mosaic designs for the basilica of San Marco, where he must have seen gold mosaic inlay of this kind.

Photomicrographs of cross-sections of paint samples from Tintoretto's 'Adoration of the Golden Calf' and 'Last Judgment'

Photographed at a magnification of approximately 100 × under the microscope

I The Adoration of the Golden Calf

a) Blue dress of woman lower left
Layer (1) (Gesso ground missing)
    2 Lead white underpaint
    3 Thin line of smalt and carbon black in discoloured oil medium
    4 Natural ultramarine + lead white

b) Bright yellow dress, foreground
Layer (1) (Gesso ground missing)
    2 Lead white underpaint
    3 Thin line of deep red lake pigment
    4 Deep yellow orpiment

II The Last Judgment

a) Blue drapery of woman, foreground
Layer 1 Gesso ground (fragment)
    2 Lead white + ochre
    3 Yellow-brown ochre with scattered multi-coloured pigment particles
    4 Multi-coloured coarse granular paint with ochre, vermilion, azurite and some lead white
    5 Pale fawn layer with mixed ochre pigments and lead white (of which a large lump is visible). This layer could be flesh paint
    6 Natural ultramarine + lead white
    7 Glaze of pure ultramarine blue
    8 Discoloured varnish (now removed from picture surface)

b) Highlight on water, foreground
Layer 1 Gesso ground
    2 Lead white underpainting with a few red particles
    3 Very thick grey-green layer packed with blue azurite and green malachite particles, lead white, and charcoal black (of which a large splinter-shaped fragment is seen right)
    4 Dark brown-green glaze
    5 Greyish-white highlight
    6 Discoloured varnish (now removed from picture surface)

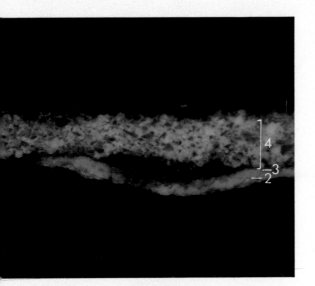

I *The Adoration of the Golden Calf*
a) Blue dress of woman pointing finger, lower left.

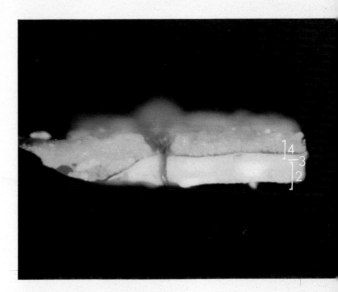

I *The Adoration of the Golden Calf*
b) Bright yellow of robe of figure, second row up.

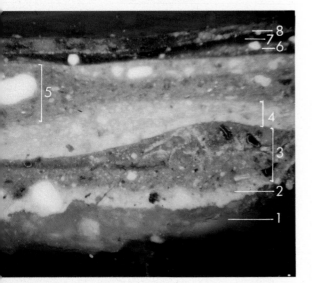

II *The Last Judgment*
a) Blue of drapery, female figure in foreground.

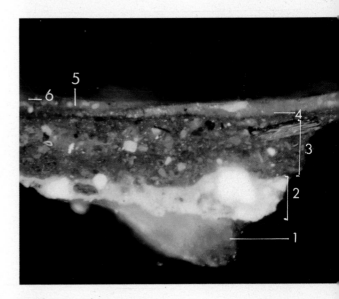

II *The Last Judgment*
b) Highlight on water, foreground.

A select bibliography of the art and history of the Madonna dell'Orto

Bigaglia, Giuseppe, *La Chiesa della Madonna dell'Orto di Venezia*, Venice, 1937

Boschini, Marco, *Le Minere della Pittura*, Venice, 1664, pp. 444–55. (Includes an account of the Scuola dei Mercanti.)

Cicogna, E. A., *Delle Iscrizioni Veneziane*, Vol. II, Venice, 1827, pp. 219–353. (A description and explanation of all inscriptions, including many now lost, both in the church and the cloister.)

Gallo, Rodolfo, 'Andrea Palladio a Venezia', *Rivista di Venezia*, 1955, pp. 36–41. (*Re* Palladio's part in the building of the Scuola dei Mercanti.)

Invernizzi, Vittorio, 'Lavori alla Chiesa della Madonna dell'Orto di Venezia', *Bollettino d'Arte*, ser. III, I, 1931–32, pp. 232–37.

Lorenzetti, Guilio, *Venice and its Lagoon*, Eng. edition, trans. by John Guthrie, Rome, 1961, (reprinted, Trieste, 1975), pp. 408–12.

Mariacher, Giovanni, *Antonio Rizzo*, (*I Maestri della Scultura*, 35), Milan, 1966. (*Re* the façade sculptures of the *Annunciation*.)

Mercati, Angelo, *La Mostra del Tintoretto*, fasc. ii, April 1937, pp. 1–6. (*Re* Tintoretto's organ doors for the church).

——, 'Storici, critici dell'arte e documenti a proposito di una pala di Palma il Vecchio', *Rendiconti. Atti della Pontificia Accademia Romana di Archeologia*, XV, 1939, pp. 21–35. (*Re* the construction and decoration of the Valier chapel.)

Palluchini, Anna, 'Considerazioni sui grandi teleri del Tintoretto della Madonna dell'Orto', *Arte Veneta*, XXIII, 1969, pp. 54–68. (*Re* Tintoretto's *Last Judgment* and *The Adoration of the Golden Calf*.) (Further bibliography of the church.)

Paoletti, Pietro, *L'Architettura e La Scultura del Rinascimento in Venezia*, Parte Iª, Venice, 1893, pp. 53–55. (*Re* the façade and portal of the church.)

Ridolfi, Carlo, *Le Maraviglie dell'Arte* (1st published 1648), ed. von Hadeln, Berlin, 1914, II, pp. 11–77, esp. 19–21. (*Re* Tintoretto and the Madonna dell'Orto.)

Sansovino, Francesco, *Venetia. Città Nobilissima*, Venice, 1581, pp. 59a–60b. (The earliest description of the church and its contents.)

Sanudo, Marin, *Miscellanea per una Cronaca Veneta*, MS., Biblioteca Correr, Venice, Cod. Cic. 970, p. 168. (For the story of the miraculous 'Madonna of the Orchard'.)

Schulz, Juergen, 'A forgotten chapter in the early history of *quadratura* painting: the fratelli Rosa', *Burlington Magazine*, ciii, 1961, pp. 90–102. (A detailed account of the work of the Rosa brothers.)

Vasari, Giorgio, *Le Vite*, ed. G. Milanesi, Vol. VI, Florence, 1881, pp. 509–10. (A description, which occurs in the Life of Garofalo, of the Rosa brothers' ceiling in the church.)

Zanetti, Vincenzo, *La Chiesa della Madonna dell'Orto in Venezia*, Venice, 1870.

Zorzi, Alvise, *Venezia Scomparsa*, II, Milan, n.d., pp. 559–61. (*Re* the Scuola dei Mercanti.)

The Committee of the Italian Art and Archives Rescue Fund

National Gallery, Trafalgar Square, London WC2

1966–1970

Chairman	Sir Ashley Clarke
Hon. Treasurer	Anthony Tuke Esq
Appeal Chairman	Mrs Peter Thorneycroft
Secretary	Mrs Humphrey Brooke

Committee

T. S. R. Boase Esq
Sir Maurice Bowra
H. N. Blakiston Esq
Sir Anthony Blunt
The Lord Bridges
Sir Kenneth Clark
The Earl of Crawford and Balcarres
The Earl of Drogheda
Sir Frank Francis
Professor Grimes
The Earl of Harewood
Sir Philip Hendy
Henry Moore Esq
John Pope-Hennessy Esq
The Lord Robbins
Professor Nicolai Rubinstein
Sir Evelyn Shuckburgh
Ellis Waterhouse Esq
Sir Charles Wheeler
Professor J. H. Whitfield

Index

Photographic credits

Cover: *Presentation of the Virgin*, Italian Art and Archives Rescue Fund; frontispiece: Venice in Peril Fund; Marco Bisà, plate 21; Osvaldo Böhm 3, 7, 67; Ashley Clarke, 8; Prince Clary von Aldringen, 11; Enzo Fassi, 13, 14, 15, 16, 22, 26, 27, 34, 35, 39, 49, 50; National Gallery, London, 92, 93, Ia, Ib, IIa, IIb; Sarah Quill, 2, 4; Fulvio Roiter, 59; *Soprintendenza ai Monumenti*, Venice, title page drawing, 1, 5, 6, 9, 10, 17, 18, 19, 20, 23, 29, 30, 31, 32, 33, 36, 37, 38, 40, 45, 46, 47, 48, 51; *Soprintendenza alle Gallerie ed Opere d'Arte*, Venice, 12, 24, 25, 28, 41, 42, 43, 44, 52, 53, 54, 55, 56, 57, 58, 60, 61, 62, 63, 64, 65, 66, 68, 69, 70, 71, 72, 73, 74, 75, 76, 77, 78, 79, 80, 81, 82, 83, 84, 85, 86, 87, 88, 89, 94, 95, 96, 97, 98, 99, 100, 101, 102, 103; the diagrams of plates 90, 91, by Lorenzo Lazzarini.

Back of Jacket. The Inscription commemorating the restoration of the church by the Italian Art and Archives Rescue Fund, assisted by the Italian government, which has been placed in the chapel to the right of the high altar